THE WELL
ADORNED
HOME

Making Luxury Livable

by Cathy Kincaid
written with Chesie Breen

Foreword by Bunny Williams and John Rosselli

RIZZOLI
NEW YORK

New York · Paris · London · Milan

Foreword

*One of my favorite possessions is a pair of red felt slippers—a gift from Cathy—that arrived
at the rehab facility I was stuck in after a fall. They cheered me up immediately,
and I got so many comments when trying to get down the hall on my walker. I know they helped
me have a speedy recovery and I still treasure them, as I do Cathy's friendship.* —John Rosselli

A number of years ago I went into John's shop and found out to my horror that most of the good things in the shop were on hold. I immediately questioned dearest Lindsay, John's wonderful assistant, as to who had them reserved, only to find out that it was her mother, Cathy Kincaid, who I had heard of but never met. Please introduce us I asked. So the next time Cathy was in town, Lindsay called, and I rushed down to John's shop to meet her (my office is in the same building). I am not sure who I fell in love with first— Cathy or her enchanting travel companion, a fluffy white dog named Daisy. It was hard to tell which end was which, as Daisy's girlish figure had expanded due to her love I found out of McDonald's drive-thru. Somehow, Cathy managed to tuck her under the seat of the plane for her frequent shopping trips to New York. So, Cathy, John, and I became dear friends and I came to admire her, not only for her beautiful design work, but also her devotion to her family, her love of animals (dogs, cats, chickens, rabbits), her energy, her humor, her curiosity, her style, and her generosity.

Cathy's work amplifies her personality. It is warm, inviting, stylish, and luxurious. Her rooms are filled with well-thought-out and original details, beautiful furniture, wonderful color combinations, and delicious fabrics. Every detail is considered, furniture perfectly arranged and special pieces chosen to give magic to her rooms. I only hope that from now on, I can get into the shops before Cathy arrives or I don't stand a chance. —**Bunny Williams**

Introduction

My childhood was spent growing up in Fort Worth, Texas, in a house filled with antiques and comfortable furnishings. As an only child, to make up for my lack of siblings and pets, I created a rich fantasy world of make-believe. Whenever I would beg my mother for a brother or sister, she would instead get me a new pet—my first was a dachshund nicknamed Chiquita. It's no surprise that I went on to have four children, who have blessed me with six grandchildren, and a menagerie of dogs, cats, and even chickens.

I inherited a love of collecting from my mother. We would use her favorite china for special occasions, and it was left to me to wash it afterward as she feared someone else would break it. How I dreaded this china. Now it's my favorite—soft gray roses with a pale robin's-egg blue and gold "pearl-like" trim.

I went on to study interior design at Texas Christian University. My first job was for Minton-Corley, the reigning firm in Fort Worth at that time. Joe Minton and David Corley's clients were among the most prominent in Texas, and their work was a mainstay in *Architectural Digest* magazine. The vogue then was to photograph projects at night with all of the lights on and candles burning. If the client wouldn't let us shoot at night, blue film was taped onto the windows. (This was long before Photoshop.)

The most important thing Joe taught me was to "imperfectly" match colors. I would work for hours trying to get all of the palettes to align and he would walk by on his way out of the office and say, "Cathy, you've got it all wrong. Create some tension. Mix up the colors. Don't try so hard to get everything to match." These words became invaluable, and when asked today how I describe myself beyond that of decorator, I answer, "Colorist."

I went on to apprentice with the Yale-educated architect and designer John Astin Perkins in Dallas, who was also one of the most influential architects and designers working in the region. He had a fearless use of color and highbrow taste, which blended to create a signature look that defined the decorating style in Dallas through the 1960s and 1970s. There were lots of fine antiques, Coromandel screens, bold palettes, tables filled with oriental figures, and accessories collected from around the world. The look was confident and sophisticated,

OPPOSITE: New painted cockpen chairs from De Angelis, upholstered in a neutral stripe, are a welcome departure from the brown wood furniture in the dining room. The elegant porcelain compote echoes the hand-painted chinoiserie panel behind it.

and everyone wanted it. John taught me to mix periods and styles, and he further developed my eye for using color in unexpected combinations.

In 1978, I struck out on my own and launched Cathy Kincaid Interiors. I was twenty-five years old at the time and in the midst of raising twins with more children to come. Balancing a career and family is difficult for most. I always felt fortunate to have a job that allowed me to attend my children's school functions and pursue interests beyond interior design. Clients benefit from a happy decorator. All of my clients have been by word of mouth. My first was a teacher that I had in high school. I have worked with many of them on several projects. One home profiled in the book is the first redecoration after thirty years. The client and I agreed at our age there probably would not be the opportunity to revisit it in another thirty years.

When I married a second time, to Bill Hudson, we purchased a storied house on Mockingbird Lane once owned by the famous Dallas designer and artist Nena Claiborne. I lovingly decorated this charming dwelling and treated every room like a jewel box, keeping many of the original design elements in place, including the dining room murals that Nena had painted. Unfortunately, tragedy struck. Bill got sick and I became a widow. And then, in 2012, just before the holidays, the house caught fire. All I grabbed while escaping the flames were my animals, and most of my personal effects were destroyed. Afterwards, I did salvage Nena's dripping wet murals, and later reinstalled them in my current house with the help of the most talented painters in Dallas, who work for Barry A. Martin Painting Contractors. As I watched everything burn, all I could think was that I was lucky. I got out safely and so did my pets. My baby granddaughter, who had been scheduled to visit the next day and sleep in a bedroom that caught fire, wasn't harmed. I chose not to rebuild: A different home would be a clean slate where I could start over. It was a chance for new beginnings. I focused on my family and continued to grow my business.

A benchmark moment in my career came when I was asked to participate in *Southern Accents'* Show House in 2003. I was tasked with designing the entire twelve-thousand-square-foot Dallas-based house with architect Robbie Fusch, who drew inspiration from the Périgord region of France. Our team had nine months to take the house from blueprints to the installation of sixteen camera-ready rooms—just like a baby. At the time *Southern Accents* was edited by Karen Carroll, and we often worked with Lydia Somerville and Clinton Smith, who was an intern. An early supporter of my work, Clint went on to become the editor-in-chief of *Veranda*, where he published many of the projects featured in this book.

Another show house I loved being involved with is the Kips Bay Decorator Show House, which benefits the Kips Bay Boys & Girls Club of New York. My dear friend Bunny Williams has chaired the show house since 2015, and it was an honor to be selected with so many talented designers. I was assigned a guest bedroom, and my first stop was John Rosselli & Associates, where I found an exquisite Anglo-Indian–style bed in ebony and bone, which I canopied in Claremont fabrics custom-embroidered by Penn & Fletcher and dressed in Leontine Linens. We covered the walls in my favorite Adelphi paper and painted the ceiling a high-gloss shade of pink from Farrow & Ball. To cool down the warm pink tones, I placed blue-and-white porcelain throughout.

I'm often asked to describe my style and the design principles that have informed me throughout my career. First, color is the foundation of all good design, be it beige, blue, or primary. If pressed to describe my forte, I think of myself first and foremost as a colorist. I begin a discussion with a client by choosing a dominant color to connect the rooms, and then repeat it in different ways throughout a home's design scheme. There is no color palette I love more than blue and white because it is soothing and works in any scenario. Paint should always be brushed on, never sprayed, including on ceilings as well as walls. I like ceilings lacquered as smooth as glass, which requires a lot of prep work but is worth it—the reflection of light from candles and chandeliers is exquisite.

As for a design's overall scheme, we pay attention to details, both small and large, and I like to mix it up. I take the time to

OPPOSITE: This second incarnation of the intimate library makes it more modern. Thirty years ago, it was decorated in English chintz, and classical oil paintings hung on the walls. We gave the room a fresh look with rich lacquered cantaloupe walls, comfortable furnishings—such as the Arne Jacobson Egg chair—and contemporary art, mixed with existing traditional furnishings and rugs.

ensure that patterns, wallpapers, textiles, furniture, and accessories are seamlessly blended. Layering is essential to creating a harmonious and uniform design. We like to use pattern everywhere for impact. Applying pattern throughout creates a less busy effect than using pieces of it randomly here and there. Colors and patterns are a great way to unite contrasting textiles and to maintain cohesion. I don't associate my work with a particular period, though you could best describe it as Anglo-American. The one aspect of design I strictly adhere to is mixing the old with the new, the ornate with the simple, and the refined with the rustic. We embrace dressmaker details, custom fabrics, antique textiles, sumptuous embroidery, and hand-painted wallpapers. When blending disparate elements, you've got to pay attention to scale and color to make sure they play well together.

Having said this, comfort and suitability are mainstays in the rooms I design. Everyone wants to have nice things, but houses are meant to be lived in and I'm insistent they feel cozy and appropriate for the clients and their lifestyle. I advise clients to buy the best they can afford—whether it be furniture, design elements, or accessories—not for investment or resale projections, but rather for quality and timelessness.

Lighting sets the tone in all of our jobs, and clients are frequently amazed at how critical it is to establish an inviting ambience. To this end, we also like to use mirrors, especially in more formal settings, but we do so when they reflect a beautiful chandelier, artwork, or an exotic antique. They also add depth to a room.

And finally, we repeat, "Edit, edit, edit," and I constantly chant to myself: Take time, relax, and enjoy the work.

LEFT: My guest room is the perfect example of a mix of high and low. I purchased the Albert Hadley–designed bed at an auction. It is flanked by Serena & Lily nightstands and topped with white Pottery Barn lamps. The custom white and pale blue Leontine Linens bedding nicely complements the Lisa Fine Textiles bed drapery. The "Besos"(or "Kisses") pillow, made by my friends at Mi Golondrina, adds a charming finishing touch to the bed.

A 1920s Spanish Colonial

Respecting Charm, Integrity, and Original Scale
When Restoring an Iconic House for Modern Living

When restoring an older home originally designed with a series of small rooms, it can be tempting to knock down walls to create larger spaces. With this house, my client, who moved to Dallas from Santa Barbara, California, was dedicated to respecting the original scale. We were influenced by Casa del Herrero, a Spanish Colonial designed by architect George Washington Smith in 1925. Here, we worked with architect Wilson Fuqua to gut every room, leaving the size the same, keeping original fireplaces, and adding custom millwork, hardware, and often tile work, making everything suitable for modern living. The decorating took its cues from the intimate scale that remained and blends the authentic spirit of this iconic house with my client's impeccable taste. Most people would have torn the house down. Instead, it has been made a better version of its original self. One reason not to demolish it was the storied past of the residence, which was once owned by Betty Blake, founder of the Dallas Museum for Contemporary Arts, and another former owner, who had a small train that ran around the property.

In the foyer, which opens to the dining room, living room, and library, a central staircase with inset tiles was added. In the house's previous incarnation, the steps were awkwardly placed coming off the kitchen. We found a pair of antique, carved confessional doors and used them to create a dramatic entrance to the Portuguese-tiled dining room. Above the doors we used an old Indian table to create a transom, giving the entry space and adjoining dining room the dose of European flourish it needed. Her collection of blue-and-white porcelain inspired the color palette, and we worked with textile designer Lisa Fine to design a custom fabric for the curtains. The walls are painted in one of my all-time favorite neutrals—Farrow & Ball Clunch.

The living room remained primarily the same. This is the only space that was expansive in size, so we divided it into intimate seating groups. We restored the windows, eliminating the stained glass that made the space dark. My clients' collection of blue-and-white porcelain mixes with a Helen Frankenthaler

OPPOSITE: The exquisite antique blue-and-white Portuguese hand-painted tile wainscoting was installed on the dining room walls. The unique antique display shelf and marble-topped wood console beautifully highlight the owner's blue-and-white porcelain collection. The hand-painted wooden lamps are topped with pleated lampshades by Charles Birdsong in a blue-and-white Robert Kime fabric.

painting on one wall and a nineteenth-century French canvas screen on the opposite wall.

The homeowners only use the library in the evening, often with a lit fire. To keep it cozy, we lacquered the walls in a cantaloupe color and chose an olive hue for the curtains, making this room a getaway from the blue-and-white palette in the formal rooms.

The kitchen, breakfast room, china pantry, and adjoining sun porch work in tandem. In these rooms, my clients' vast collections of fine china, creamware, and drab ware are happily displayed. Geometric tiles mixed with more modern furniture in the sunroom pick up Moroccan aspects woven throughout the home.

The house is designed to expand when needed or become more intimate when it is just the two of them. Upstairs is a series of carefully appointed bedrooms and the master suite, where soft blues pair with a neutral shell of dusty pink. A custom Anglo-Indian–style canopy bed is dressed in Penny Morrison fabrics and Leontine Linens, and a subtly patterned wall covering is from Adelphi. The soft colors and nuanced patterns throughout the interior spaces speak to one another instead of colliding.

The back house was newly added to accommodate modern conveniences not suitable for the home's historical footprint. This addition both preserves and continues the original architecture's best feature—its timeless sense of intimate scale. Connected by tucked brickwork and archways, the new structure houses a guest suite, home office, music room, spa, and gym.

The house is successful and beloved for many reasons though mostly because of my clients' dedication to historic preservation. The couple, respectful of its original spirit, retained much of the architectural detail. My goal was to apply the same level of thought and care to the decorating.

RIGHT: This is the only room original to the house. The expansive Doris Leslie Blau blue-and-white rug sets the tone for the space with multiple comfortable and inviting seating areas. Farrow & Ball Ammonite paint on the walls provides the perfect backdrop for the clients' twentieth-century art and nineteenth-century French canvas screen.

ABOVE: A pair of awkward corners has been fitted with two small matching banquettes, covered in a blue-and-white Bennison stripe fabric. The banquettes and a small wooden armchair in a Fortuny textile provide additional seating for parties. OPPOSITE: Careful furniture selection and placement make this intimate library multifunctional, with an antique wooden and leather-topped desk, a cozy chair and ottoman, and a full drinks tray ready for entertaining. The upholstered chair and ottoman, and the roman shades are in a Claremont fabric. The rug is a Stark sisal.

OPPOSITE: Intricate architectural details and a nineteenth-century light fixture create a whimsical, yet practical, dish pantry, perfect for displaying some of the clients' china and silver collection. The antique textile curtain hides storage below.

BLUE-AND-WHITE TILE WORK

We used blue-and-white tile throughout this Spanish Mediterranean house but nowhere more boldly than in the dining room. In lieu of a traditional chair rail, blue-and-white Portuguese tiles from Solar Antique Tiles create a bold border and complement to the clients' collection of blue-and-white porcelain and curtains in Lisa Fine Textiles mixed with Robert Kime fabrics. I consider the combination of blue and white to be a neutral and apply it as such, especially when it comes to porcelain.

LEFT: Antique Portuguese convent doors with a carved panel from a Syrian table function as a transom leading into the dining room. The eclectic mix of styles in the room—from an English nineteenth-century table and painted Regency chairs to a Syrian mirror and French Empire chandelier—are harmonized by the blue-and-white textiles. The drapery fabric by Lisa Fine Textiles was custom-designed to complement the tile wainscot.

OPPOSITE: The layering of patterns in this bright and happy solarium provides interest and warmth in what otherwise could have been a cold room. The comfortable Kisabeth banquette, upholstered in a Claremont fabric, with antique textile pillows, lends a bohemian feel, as does the blue, white, and gray Ann Sacks floor tile in a tumbling blocks pattern.

RIGHT: Bedrooms should be luxurious, yet functional. Inside the bed drapery, lamps on swing arms, shaded with bespoke antique textile lampshades by Charles Birdsong, provide ample reading light. A bedside table, with room for storage and a pullout shelf for water and a phone, is both pretty and useful.

ABOVE: Bathrooms must be practical, yet they can also be attractive. Architectural details and high-gloss paint for durability are key elements. Embroidered café curtains from Julia B. and monogrammed towels from Matouk are lovely accents. OPPOSITE: This nautical-inspired spa features custom-made blue-and-white tiles by Ann Sacks. A deck chair provides a place to relax in this calming sanctuary.

A Jewel-Box Pied-à-Terre

*Making Small Rooms Big Through
Balance, Symmetry, and Scale*

If you were to picture the quintessential pied-à-terre, this 1,100-square-foot Fifth Avenue apartment with wraparound terraces overlooking Central Park in a Rosario Candela and James Carpenter building is the poster child. The client started by enlisting architect John B. Murray to make the small spaces big. Beautiful, newly designed classical moldings helped raise the ceilings, and a clever use of mirrored panels opened up the spaces and offered the perfect backdrop for me to go about decorating. Another trick for making small spaces feel bigger is to lacquer ceilings in pale blue to give the illusion of sky. We did this throughout, and then we did what we do best: We layered the decor without going overboard. When decorating small spaces, the more you add, the less busy it can seem.

In the living room, my client opted to keep the Zuber wall murals because she felt they spoke to the provenance of the space, and I agreed. However, there was a decorative balustrade that ran beneath them and gave the room a 1980s hangover. We replaced it with wood paneling in a subdued lacquer finish, which made the space feel crisper and less dowdy. There are a number of dressmaker details in this room, such as pleated lampshades and curtains with custom trim. These elements mix with silver chandeliers, gilded frames, and the blue-and-white porcelain I never tire of. What keeps the room from seeming chaotic is strict attention to balance, scale, and symmetry. Notice there are a lot of pairs in the form of lamps, brackets, sconces, and chairs, and the two seating areas in the living room are equally weighted in importance. One is for dining and the other is for visiting, offering an unexpected form of symmetry and balance.

A narrow hallway with a lacquered, robin's-egg blue vaulted ceiling and a hanging grid of antique botanical prints in black and white connects the formal front room to the bedroom suite, which is comprised of a master bedroom, sitting room, and his-and-hers baths. A subtly patterned pale robin's-egg blue-and-white fabric by Penny Morrison covers the furniture, walls, and windows in the sitting room, creating a cozy nook with a trundled daybed. An antique writing desk perched between two windows with views to Central Park makes this the perfect place to work.

The husband is a sailor so when designing his bath, the architect treated it like the head on a boat with polished mahogany and white marble. A boat's ceiling is wooden shiplap, so Corian was used to create a pattern that would trick the eye into thinking it was shiplap.

Another trick for small spaces is to use one pattern throughout, as in the aforementioned sitting room. Most people think that pattern will overwhelm a room. That can happen if a pattern is used piecemeal, but the opposite is true when there's continuity. In the master bedroom, we opted for a bold, outsize paisley in lilac and used it on nearly every surface.

In the end, with the triumvirate of the client, architect, and me, we were able to strip away the stodgy elements and create a beautifully tailored and well-proportioned apartment by challenging ourselves to achieve balance, symmetry, and scale, blended with pattern, soft color, and dressmaker details.

OPPOSITE AND FOLLOWING SPREAD: The chinoiserie secretary displays the clients' collection of miniature blue-and-white Chinese export garniture and a bronze doré clock. To achieve the intimacy of the penthouse living room, meticulous planning was required. Due to the clever design of drapery pockets by architect John B. Murray, the drapery has been integrated into the moldings, which extend to the ceiling to give the illusion of height. To accommodate as much seating as possible, the comfortable furniture has been scaled down.

THE POWER OF PAIRS

We've always believed in layering in detail in small spaces. What saves them from feeling cluttered is pairing, whether in seating groups, lighting, or decorative objects. Here, we have used pairs in unexpected ways while still giving order to what could otherwise read as chaos.

OPPOSITE: Mirrors and lighting create the magic for this tiny entry. Always use scaled-down furniture in small spaces.

RIGHT: With careful editing, small spaces can be layered with details, and yet not feel cluttered. One way to accomplish this is with pairings. In this room, we used pairs of chairs, lamps, and accessories.

LEFT: We removed the dowdy wainscoting from below the existing wallpaper, and the architect designed an elegant paneled wainscot. Crown molding was installed to raise the ceilings. A seating alcove was designed to double as a glamorous dining area in the evening or a cozy spot to have breakfast or work during the day.

37

OPPOSITE: In the living room where the walls are densely patterned, solids were used for upholstery and drapery to add a layer of calm. The adjacent hallway's walls are "papered" with framed botanicals to create a paneled effect.

OPPOSITE: A large-scale paisley, chosen by the client, makes the small bedroom seem larger. Plates hung over the fireplace are a departure from expected artwork. A bracket adds dimension to this grouping of blue-and-white porcelain. ABOVE: The elegant built-in daybed designed by the architect, along with the shelves, created a perfect space to use the same fabric for this versatile and handsome room. We like to finish wallpaper or fabric with a narrow ribbon trim.

ABOVE: The client is an accomplished sailor. Therefore, the architect designed this intimate bathroom as a ship captain's bath, complete with nautical instruments. A V-groove Corian ceiling was used to resemble wood—it allows for easy upkeep. OPPOSITE: When drawn up, the Roman shades reveal the wonderful view of Central Park. The Christopher Spitzmiller lamp lights this simple, elegant work space.

A Ship Captain's Cottage

Seamlessly Blending a Historic Structure with the Addition of Master and Guest Suites

When my clients purchased this picturesque ship captain's house dating back to the 1750s, it was to fulfill the wife's desire to spend more time on the East Coast, where she was originally from. The cottage was brimming with charm, which we wanted to preserve, but it wasn't really suitable for modern family living. Our goal was to respect its provenance—which meant low ceilings, small passageways and room sizes, steep stairways to attic rooms, and dark paneling—while making it more comfortable and livable. The house perches on a hill that sweeps down to the Connecticut River, where the husband moors his motor yacht. To capture the magical sense of place, we also paid careful attention to the outdoor spaces, which include a dovecote, pool, porches, potting shed, vegetable garden, and a traditional red barn.

Our two grandest gestures for modernizing the house include the addition of an upstairs master suite above the living room and a new entrance and double-height entry foyer with a wall of paneled windows and wooden staircase leading to a well-appointed guest suite with a large bathroom, reading nook, and walk-in closet. These two structures allowed the house to breathe, making the smaller, cozy rooms feel less cramped.

For the house's color palette, we worked with sage greens, muddy reds, mustard yellows, and soft blues. We kept the new entry spare to enhance its modern sensibility and furnished the space with a painted American settee and a large Swedish table holding a pair of blue-and-white lamps. In the original entry hall, we preserved the wood paneling and hung my clients' collection of porcelain, drabware, and artwork. Down the hall are the living room, dining room, front parlor, and two bedrooms—all original to the house. A modern kitchen was incorporated. The living room, anchored by a large fireplace, has multiple seating groups and a little corner banquette for a quiet meal or a spot to work on a puzzle. The dining room with an oval-shaped table opposite the original fireplace and sitting room for after-dinner visits is paneled and painted sage green. The front parlor is used mostly for reading. These clients rarely watch television, so every room is designed to encourage conversation, reading, games, and quality family time.

The front bedroom, furnished with two twin beds with upholstered headboards and a bedside table tucked between, looks out to the river. An original set of stairs off the kitchen leads to an attic bedroom.

A series of gated walkways and gardens surround the house and lead to a sunken pool and accompanying dovecote. More recently, a vegetable garden and potting shed were added next to a traditional New England red barn. There are porches on the sides and front of the house, which help expand its footprint. During the warm weather, most meals are served on a tented pitch off the kitchen and dining room with views over pasture, and the river.

Today, this house has the perfect balance of old-fashioned charm and modern sensibility. It is successful because we were careful to respect the importance of both elements without letting one take control.

OPPOSITE: A large window in this otherwise small cottage brings the outdoors inside. Wide plank floors and a simple balustrade reinforce the country feel of this new addition. The large Dutch chandelier with custom shades casts a warm light over the space. The most important member of the household, Ferris, is ready to greet whoever arrives.

RIGHT: Les Indiennes fabric on all the walls and Roman shades turn this tiny library into a cozy enclave. The chair and ottoman are upholstered in Pierre Frey's Le Manach. The fabric's borders have been utilized for the cushion boxing and skirt borders.

FOLLOWING SPREAD: The family room is equally inviting in the summer or winter thanks to the floral chintz in greens, browns, and blues. Antique textiles are used for pillows. An antique bamboo corner chair has a custom-made cushion made from a vintage sari. A pale blue Elizabeth Eakins rug in a soft blue wool is a neutral backdrop for all the pattern.

RIGHT: For a cozy corner in the dining room, we used a Sister Parish fabric for the drapery and custom-colored Bennison fabric for the sofa. I prefer custom fabrics because they give a client a unique design.

OPPOSITE: Tables that expand are the best for any dining room, especially for a small one like this. The striped cotton rug from Elizabeth Eakins is perfect for this country look. Dining room chairs should be comfortable so that guests will linger at the table. These balloon-back chairs that we custom designed add color and pattern to this room.

COLLECTING AND STORAGE

I have an affinity for collecting antique porcelain and pottery, which this client shares with gusto. She prefers to hang her collection, and we did so in every room. We built out this butler's pantry to store her treasures, which she often rotates.

LEFT: Farrow & Ball Olive Green is the perfect backdrop for the giltwood frame and the drabware plate in the dining room. The nautical motif on the antique clock echoes the theme of the ship captain's cottage.

OPPOSITE: An Adelphi paper lines this tiny butler's pantry, where the client's collection of her mother's china is displayed. The cranberry red of the glassware is picked up in the wallpaper pattern. For someone who collects china, a dish pantry such as this is a must.

OPPOSITE: Details are so important in all rooms, especially a bedroom.
Bespoke lampshades—some in patterned fabrics—are used, even in the lantern
that prevents glare. Julia B. eyelet linens and embroidered pillows layer the bed.

OPPOSITE: The cozy upstairs guest room has custom wallpaper by Adelphi with a contrasting trim. The bed is dressed in a custom Chelsea Textiles fabric that is used as a border to outline the headboard. Simple curtains on iron rods and rings finish this room. ABOVE: A window seat tucked in the end of a hallway is the perfect way to bring in light and create a focal point. Tissus d'Hélène fabric in a small border stripe is the right scale for this diminutive space.

ABOVE AND OPPOSITE: The mix of patterns in the Robert Kime wallpaper and the Jasper fabric on the drapery, headboard, and the custom lampshade contribute to keeping this guest room from becoming ordinary. Headboards can be any shape—this gothic design is one of our favorites. The bone lamp from John Rosselli & Associates is small enough not to take over the bedside table's surface. I always provide a luggage rack in guest rooms. This charming Colefax and Fowler rack, covered in one of their iconic fabrics, has ribbon straps.

OPPOSITE: A breakfast on the terrace is served on a McKinnon and Harris table with matching chairs. McKinnon and Harris, based in Richmond, Virginia, has some of the best examples of American-made furniture. ABOVE: This structure, called the "The Birdhouse," was designed to be a pool cabana or a spot for suppers and cocktails. The banquettes are covered in a Lisa Fine Textiles bird-motif fabric, and there are framed bird engravings on the walls.

RIGHT: The table is set for a lovely lunch on this Turkish classic wood yacht. Delany & Long pale blue fabric on the banquettes and Kravet yellow ikat on the pillows are elegant, yet durable, performance fabrics. The nautical theme is carried through in the napkins and the silver lighthouse cocktail shaker.

FOLLOWING SPREAD: Classic blue-and-white is the color scheme for the yacht's stateroom. The floor is covered in Stark's Les Damian carpet, and the chairs are upholstered in Brunschwig & Fils's Digby's Tent, which is also used for the pillows.

A Storied Family Residence

Brightening a 1920s Tudor House for a Stylish Family with a Nod to Iconic American Decorators

One of the first challenges we faced with this project was knowing what to strip away architecturally and what to add in its place. The original architect for this house was Hal Thomson—a parallel is a John Staub house in Houston or a David Adler house in the Midwest. This house is beautifully detailed and laid out, but the interiors were very somber. There were small leaded-glass windows everywhere, drab plaster walls, and dark brown woodwork. We worked with Dallas-based architect Wilson Fuqua, and often joked that we "neutered the Tudor."

The main mission was to lighten, brighten, and conjure the relaxed elegance of an English country house with an East Coast sensibility for a young couple with three children. Wilson has renovated several Thomson houses and gets the credit for opening up the house. We were committed to retaining the original brick and stonework but, as with most Tudor houses, the windows were small resulting in dark rooms. These windows came out and were replaced with much larger ones that now flood the rooms with light throughout the house. The addition of a strong dose of white trim work brightens the facade.

Another bold architectural gesture was to double the size of the solarium and link it to the enclosed porch with steel casement doors. Today, this is the room where everyone gravitates. The house's interior design needed to set the tone for the way this family lives and entertains. As this family is not pretentious in anyway, we wanted the decor to remind everyone that it was okay to be playful.

I was inspired by the treillage design after visiting Bunny Mellon's former Manhattan townhouse, which was purchased by a friend. What's unique about this trelliswork is the lattice is oval and therefore there are no sharp edges. It is not broken up by competing design elements. The trelliswork adds depth and dimension without being fussy. It is delicate and refined with a whimsical aspect that cheers up the space.

The upholstery is covered in one of my favorite chintzes, which makes the room look unified and calm, even though it is a big print. Rather than using a fabric that was bright and contemporary for this young family, we chose a Robert Kime chintz in muted colors that imparts a traditional feeling without being stuffy. The room is happy with children, friends, and dogs all feeling right at home. A circular stairway in the corner leads to a wine cellar and games room inspired by the 1770 House in East Hampton, a favorite haunt for my clients.

My clients have become more serious about collecting art, and the living room reflects some of the pieces they've become interested in, including a Pierre Bonnard that hangs above the fireplace. Again, these clients are not stuffy. They are confident mixing eclectic, contemporary pieces with nineteenth-century art.

The Anglo-Indian/American foyer murals depicting elephants, Indians, and monkeys, which moved with them from their previous house, were hand-painted by Pierre Finkelstein. Leaded-glass windows with a tree motif weave up the circular stairway.

OPPOSITE: The unique shutter design for this living room came from a Hal Thomson house that my clients once owned. The Edwardian upholstered furniture, designed by De Angelis in a Robert Kime chintz, is luxurious, yet durable.

OPPOSITE: This leaded glass window with images of trees is one of two that are original to the house. ABOVE: These panels were hand-painted by Pierre Finkelstein of New York City. They were moved from their previous home to this oval entry. FOLLOWING SPREAD: The living room walls are lined with canvas, crosshatched, and lacquered. This treatment provides a neutral backdrop for the clients, who are sophisticated art collectors, to display their collection. A Pierre Bonnard painting hanging over the mantel complements the contemporary pieces by Raphaelle Goethals on the walls.

The dining room with our signature high-gloss walls has two seating configurations—a large and formal rectangular-shaped Georgian-style table from Florian Papp and a smaller circular table in a newly added bay window overlooking the back gardens for more intimate dinners.

In the family room off the kitchen, we returned to a Robert Kime print but this time chose one with more of an Anglo-Indian flavor, which we applied onto the walls with a custom Claremont trim. Florals and stripes on the upholstery round out the room.

A back staircase floats in front of a two-story wall of windows to the second- and third-floor bedrooms. Wilson was so clever in designing this aspect—it brings much-needed light into the middle of the house and lends a contemporary element.

Everyone's favorite bedroom is the attic guest room, which is my homage to the legendary designer Sister Parish. I'm friends with her granddaughter, Susan Crater, and I once stayed in the guest room at Mrs. Parish's summerhouse in Maine. I honored her by painting the floors blue, and used her classic Dolly fabric all over the room.

The master suite, which includes the husband's office, is done in paneling in a honey-colored faux pine. So we opted for more traditional English furnishings and selected fabrics from Chelsea Textiles for a canopied bed. We used two small floral prints on the outside—Forget-Me-Not and Carnation Vine—and a small check for the interior. A pair of Colefax and Fowler lamps flanks the bed.

What could have been a stodgy and imposing house was given a new lease on life by replacing small windows with those allowing abundant light and opening up key rooms to create anchor spaces for a family with grown-up taste—and a side of whimsy.

RIGHT: A De Angelis sofa, with a mix of antique textile pillows, is an inviting place to sit. It has been placed in front of a monumental Coromandel screen, with a Gerhard Richter painting hanging in the center. FOLLOWING SPREAD: Styled by Charles Birdsong, this exquisite solarium features an artful display of watercolors of feathered birds among mismatched end tables, lamps, and porcelains.

PAYING HOMAGE TO TRELLIS

Trellis (or treillage) is an iconic American decorating technique, so the challenge is making it your own. Here, we designed the lattice on a refined diagonal that I find delicate, and then added a circular motif border and extended an elongated pattern up the lacquered walls, which curve into the ceiling.

LEFT: This lattice design was inspired by Bunny Mellon's townhouse located on New York City's Upper East Side. The carpenters were very clever in their replication of the oval lattice design. It is painted in Farrow & Ball Clunch with Farrow & Ball Pale Powder lacquered walls beneath it.

OPPOSITE: The comfortable De Angelis chairs around the game table are covered in a Veere Grenney fabric. The chair design includes a top railing with an "H" motif—which happens to be the clients' initial.

OPPOSITE: The second entry, with its floating staircase in front of a two-story steel window by Wilson Fuqua, brings an inviting feel to what otherwise could have been a dark space. ABOVE: The oval dish room allows everyone to enjoy the owner's collection of porcelain. The pullouts under the upper cabinets are a convenient surface to rest dishes on when they are removed from the shelves.

ABOVE: Dining rooms should be flexible. This small nook at the end of a rather large dining room is ideal for breakfast and intimate suppers. OPPOSITE: The lacquered ceiling and stried walls reflect the lighting, as well as candlelight, in a dining room. I find that first purchasing a rug inspires the color scheme for a room. The Chelsea Textiles drapery was custom colored to complement the Oushak rug.

RIGHT: There is almost nothing more inviting than a comfortable sofa in a window. The Robert Kime fabric on the walls with custom Claremont Indian-style trimmings is the motif that connects all the elements of the room.

OPPOSITE: Open shelves in a kitchen give easy access to dishes, oils, and spices, and help to keep items organized. The antique chandelier from a French orangery fills the lofty space. Delft tiles without the traditional blue over-pattern create a neutral background. ABOVE: If budget allows, always use reclaimed mantels. They add charm and authenticity to a room. The juxtaposition of the formal Delft garniture and the Regency table with the informal chairs is united by the inviting blue-and-white color scheme.

ABOVE: A tiny octagonal library is one of the favorite rooms in the house. People tend to gravitate to small spaces due to their intimacy. This one is especially nice since it leads to the terrace outside. OPPOSITE: This third-floor "attic guest room" is an homage to Sister Parish. I had the honor of being a guest in her house in Islesboro, Maine. The room I stayed in was decorated in this fabric and the painted blue floor was covered with an L.L. Bean hooked rug. FOLLOWING SPREAD: The inspiration for this basement is the 1770 House in East Hampton, Long Island, with its walls dressed up in vintage Zuber panels. Reclaimed antique paneling was used, and Art Deco leather chairs from the Paris flea market set the mood for enjoying wine and cigars.

A Magical Mas de Baraquet

Fulfilling a Husband's Dream of a Family Retreat in the Provençal Countryside

I could not have been more excited than when my clients called me and said they had purchased a home in Provence. I knew that had been somewhat of a dream of the husband's—a self-described Francophile—making it a dream of a project all around. This couple had become familiar with the house through many visits to that area. They knew the owners and had even been entertained in the *mas*, as they call a farmhouse in the South of France. When the owner hinted that he might be selling, it was a "done deal."

The exquisite Mas de Baraquet had been lovingly restored and rebuilt by the previous owners. It was impossible to tell where the original house was and where the restoration began. I credit the previous owners and the architect for giving me the perfect palette to create a new life for the house for the next owners. We decided to keep the fabrics simple and the art fresh and contemporary. Since this house is used mostly in the warmer months, the fabrics, rugs, and colors are more Mediterranean. Instead of traditional toile, we opted for prints reminiscent of Souleiado calicos. The first space most people enter is the solarium, which doubles as a breakfast room and casual sitting area for TV or just catching a nap. Lisa Fine Textiles fabrics in pretty greens and blues inspired this room.

In the foyer, we retained a large tapestry and painted screen from the previous owners, but once again, simple fabrics and cotton-striped rugs were used. Antique textile pillows on sofas and ethnic fabrics on chairs and lampshades add layers of detail and whimsy.

In the generously sized living room, which is surrounded outside with side gardens and fields of flowers, I wanted to provide multiple seating areas with views. But most important was the mix of styles and details. Antiques and comfortable upholstery are covered in traditional prints tempered with linen ticking and textiles to keep a mix. Plain linen drapery, all custom-embroidered by Penn & Fletcher in New York, offers lavish detail that is still appropriate for a country home. Painted furniture, Anglo-Indian inlaid pieces, midcentury Jansen chairs, and a French Deco coffee table keep the mood fresh and young. We hung dioramas, contemporary art, watercolors of birds with real feathers, and book screens found at the flea market. There is always a pleasing place for the eye to rest.

The wonderful details the architect designed include a built-in cupboard in the butler's pantry. Combined with the hand-blocked paper and ribbon trim on the walls and the checked fabric on the doors and lining the baskets, this tiny room became a wonderful pass-through to the dining room.

The overall intention of the dining room decor was a fresh approach to traditional French design. We used a refined hand-blocked paper for the walls, which contrasts with the beams. The chandelier is by a contemporary sculptor from the South of France, as is the mirror. The chairs are midcentury from the David Hicks estate and the rug is a casual striped dhurrie. The clients chose contemporary art at the Dallas Art Fair to complete this room. Peering into the cozy bar from the dining room, we used an Indian hand-blocked fabric lantern from Guinevere in London.

OPPOSITE: In the entry, the traditional provincial furniture is freshened up with solid fabrics, ikats, and simple cotton-striped dhurries. Sari lampshades on the Chinese export lamps provide a little surprise.

The contrast with the existing reclaimed piece of nineteenth-century cabinetry in the bar lends a whimsical twist to the space.

The library is a warm and inviting space between the entry and the living room. We painted the room a warm cantaloupe color instead of leaving it white like the rest of the house. Looking down the enfilade and having a glimpse of a different color is intriguing and inviting. Antique portraits and leather bindings paired with apple matting on the floors, antique textiles, and linen ikat drapery keep the library from taking itself too seriously.

The kitchen is the heart of the house with its large fireplace and ample cooking space. The wife is an accomplished cook and loves to entertain—and what better place to have the best ingredients and backdrop for fabulous meals? Nineteen-thirties French leather chairs flank the fireplace with a contemporary painting by Dallas artist David Bates of sunflowers. Not to mention, the view from the kitchen in summer months is a sunflower field.

I love to use twin beds in a room as a king bed. The two beds can be separated or left together to make a very flexible interior—especially in a vacation house. Les Indiennes stone-colored Indian cottons, neutral checks, Leontine Linens, and a casual sisal rug make this a laid-back room.

In the master bedroom, the charming architecture of this room called for a simple approach to the decoration. Aleta Anglo-Indian flower fabric was used to provide a light yet luxurious feel. A cotton antique dhurrie rug adds another pattern, and borders from a coordinating fabric are used for trim on the drapery to keep it less fussy. Small slipper chairs are placed at the end of the bed for a visitor or for placing books or night robes. Christopher Spitzmiller lamps with custom linen shades and Julia B. custom linens complete this bespoke bedroom. The master bath was designed by the architects with a nod to large baths of the eighteenth and nineteenth centuries. The tiles contrast with beautiful paneling and millwork and a contemporary suzani-patterned fabric by Penny Morrison in soft colors on the rustic chair. Using traditional light fixtures but covering shades on pricket lamps in a bright Ikat, create a happy environment for first thing in the morning or last thing in the evening.

RIGHT: Multiple seating areas are the key to a flexible living room. Midcentury tables combined with eighteenth-century chairs make this space feel fresh.

OPPOSITE: The juxtaposition of contemporary art, nineteenth-century dioramas, gothic consoles, Indian textiles, and furniture, alongside this provincial mantel, keep the room interesting and young—like the family who lives here. ABOVE: The painted legs of the 1940s Jansen slipper chairs echo the painted eighteenth-century fauteuils next to them. Chinese export blue-and-white *kraak* ware has been placed over the sofa in an arc around an eighteenth-century *tulipiere* filled with flowers.

ABOVE: The enfilade, designed by the architect Bruno Lafourcade, creates a wonderful inviting view of the house—with a glance, one can see all the rooms. OPPOSITE: I love this cantaloupe color for walls since it makes for a room that glows in a flattering way. The ikat fabric is fun next to the serious portrait of someone's ancestor. FOLLOWING SPREAD: This dining room is one of my very favorite rooms, not only due to its eclectic design elements, but also because of the wonderful dinners that my client has enjoyed here. The resin mirror and the chandelier are by local artisans from the South of France.

MODERNIZING FRENCH TRADITIONAL

Quintessential Provençal style typically conjures toile, pottery, and iron chandeliers. My clients wanted something more modern, so we removed the toile and iron and then redesigned the spaces with Anglo-Indian prints, painted furniture, simple cotton rugs, contemporary art, and more stylish lighting.

LEFT: This George Spencer hand-blocked wallpaper is the perfect backdrop for blue-and-white export china, the bone-inlaid Syrian bracket, and the bone lamp with a bespoke shade, designed by Charles Birdsong.

OPPOSITE: The Indian print floating "orb" light fixture from Guinevere in London makes this bar, which is original to the house, fun and sexy. It is a visual surprise off the dining room.

RIGHT: An important chinoiserie lantern hangs above a center table flanked with painted stools around a Biedermeier table. The stools, covered in a whimsical Penny Morrison suzani fabric, lighten the mood in the formal entry.

OPPOSITE: For this hardworking kitchen, a table from the previous owner has been converted into a useful island. The walls are lined with paintings of trophies and food, and pots and pans.

FOLLOWING SPREAD: The contemporary "sunflower" painting anchors the upstairs sitting room—a sunny afternoon retreat. A Penny Morrison block-print fabric coves all the furniture, and the floor is layered with rugs.

RIGHT: A mix of Lisa Fine Textiles fabrics on the traditional Louis XV bergères and sofa complement the contemporary paintings of citrus by Ryan Mrozowski in the orangery, giving it new life.

OPPOSITE: Using one Aleta fabric everywhere in this master bedroom creates a restful sanctuary. ABOVE: This master bath is elegant and practical at the same time, thanks to the careful planning of the architect and previous owner. The bathtub was tucked into an alcove, with storage closets on both sides.

ABOVE: This funky bathtub adds whimsy to the bathroom. An étagère is always handy next to a tub that is floating in a room, and a chair provides a convenient spot to place a robe or a towel.
OPPOSITE: Les Indiennes cottons are the perfect choice for the simple and sunny guest room. Twin beds are ideal for a guest room because of their flexibility. Here, they have been pushed together as a king, but can be easily separated when need be.

A Stately Duplex Apartment

Transitioning from a Late Twentieth-Century Tudor into a Twenty-First-Century High-Rise

When the last of my clients' five children went off to college, the wife decided to "downsize" from a larger Tudor house to a twelve-thousand-square-foot duplex in one of Dallas's newest and most prestigious high-rise buildings. Because the couple prefers smaller, more intimate rooms, we had to find ways to break up the large open spaces with walls of plated glass. We worked with architect Wilson Fuqua to humanize the grand scale of the existing spaces. Bringing the walls in enabled us to design deep window seats, and, in some rooms, we lowered the ceilings to create a sense of intimacy. My client travels extensively and has an extensive collection of antiques, especially porcelain and lighting, and she wanted to use the things she had always loved but in a fresh way. We sought to harmonize the couple's furnishings into an elegant homage to a prewar New York apartment.

As with most prewar apartments in New York, the foyer is a grand gesture and used to connect multiple rooms. Here, formal French limestone floors in a black-and-white checkerboard pattern are surrounded by walls lacquered in apple green with large hanging nineteenth-century chinoiserie panels.

The dining room blends vintage black leather chairs with an antique French table and an eighteenth-century Swedish chandelier. We added special details like a chair rail and antique mirror behind treillage to make the room feel special. In the living room, we did the same by incorporating antique pine paneling. Most would have wanted to optimize the sweeping city views but we wanted to turn the rooms inwards to create a cozy effect. The client opted for good English furniture and antiques and layered antique rugs on top of sisal, giving the room the feeling of a study in an English country house.

The music room off the foyer is one of my favorites. We created panels from an oversized patterned fabric from a Jasper Louis XI fauteuil. A mélange of art gives the space an exotic flair.

My client loves red, so it is seen throughout the house, including two places you may expect it the least—the kitchen and the bedroom. A giant island is painted tomato red and cabinets are lined in a fabric from Lisa Fine Textiles. In the bedroom, my client wanted to use her former canopy bed, so we restyled it by leaving the Chelsea Textiles on the outside but relining the inside with a punchy red-and-white check.

Even though there was so much space in the apartment, it often felt as if we were inventing rooms to make it feel like a cozy home. Though technically smaller than their Tudor house, I think we succeeded in creating warm, lively, and functional interiors without sacrificing personality. We did not want to lose the charm and intimacy of their prior life—now they can turn one lock and leave.

OPPOSITE: For this library, I chose Farrow & Ball Pantelon paint as it fit this sophisticated space. It's one of my favorite colors—not green or brown but a mixture of both.

ABOVE: The clients' Chinese panels are a perfect backdrop for an exquisite collection of furniture and accessories. OPPOSITE: Layering rugs on top of sisal makes a room feel larger and softens the space visually. The furniture in the library has been placed on sisal rugs and an antique rug. FOLLOWING SPREAD: The exquisite pine paneling for the sitting room was faux painted by Barry A. Martin Painting Contractors.

OPPOSITE: Patterned wallpaper gives walls perspective and depth. This small dining room, with walls covered in a Colfax and Fowler paper, appears much larger than it is. ABOVE: The antique mirror set above the lattice wainscot adds interest and detail to this small room.

INTRODUCING RED

Everyone knows my love of soft blues, but I also feel right at home with red. The deep red running throughout this duplex is my client's favorite color. In the kitchen, we used it unabashedly whereas in the master bedroom we tiptoed in with a Chelsea Textiles check on the interior of the canopy bed. In fact, red is peppered in most of the spaces.

LEFT: The client, who enjoys cooking, desired a thread of red throughout the house. For the kitchen, we accomplished this by lining the cabinet doors in a red fabric from Lisa Fine Textiles, which works well with the Farrow & Ball Mouse's Back paint color on the woodwork.

OPPOSITE: This windowless room, which is really a pass-through, has become a favorite due to the Indian flower panels by Michael S. Smith, which resemble windows.

LEFT: You should never be afraid to hang art on top of patterned, upholstered walls or scenic wallpaper. The layering of these engravings adds interest to the walls.

ABOVE: Her master bath in Farrow & Ball Dutch Pink with a Farrow & Ball Pale Powder ceiling has great views of the city. I always like to place a comfortable chair, in this case covered in a Robert Kime linen, in a bathroom if there is space. OPPOSITE: The painted shiplap on the ceiling complements the clients' English country bed, which was originally dressed in a blue Chelsea Textiles check. An effective way to update a room is to simply replace the entire fabric.

A Family House Reimagined

*Starting Small and Seeing the Value in
Quality Pieces with Timeless Style*

This client is an old friend who just wanted to give the house a little lift. What started as a small project ended up becoming a grand design scheme. One of the things I think my clients appreciate about me is my affinity for reusing and repurposing existing pieces. If the quality is good, the style is timeless.

So, what started as a nip and a tuck ended up being a complete redesign of the couple's house and the addition of the ultimate personal space—a "she shed." This house already had a firm foundation on which to build the design plan. There were country French overtones in the house and furniture. We diluted that look and freshened everything up so that the feeling is now more eclectic. We shopped for furniture in England and France, and of course the wonderful shops such as Nick Brock, Wolf Hall, and Ceylon et Cie in Dallas.

We brought in antique Swedish and modern pieces to bring a fresh feel to the dining and living rooms. There's a Swedish lightness to the painted chairs in the dining room paired with bleached demilune tables that work well with a soft blue palette and striped walls and rug.

To add depth to the living room, we flanked the fireplace with a pair of mirrors, giving the illusion of windows. The dusty blue palette continues and picks up shades in the existing rug. For a midcentury twist on her existing country French furniture, we added a midcentury glass-topped coffee table that gives the room a modern lift. Swedish and French accents carry over into the breakfast room area, where we hung a hand-painted textile and antique delft plates over a painted bench and drop-leaf oak table.

Upstairs in the master bedroom, we did what we love to do. We chose a Bennison hand-blocked print in red and blue and used it everywhere. The more patterns you use, the less busy it seems. My client loves linens and the beds are softly dressed in Leontine Linens and D. Porthault. She also collects blue-and-white Hatcher porcelain.

What used to be a playroom is now the upstairs sitting room with comfortable upholstery covered in a mix of Michael S. Smith, Peter Fasano, and Robert Kime fabrics. The Parsons tables are covered in wallpaper—something I do often—and were built by Barry A. Martin Painting Contractors in Dallas.

Our final flourish was to work with architect Jay Smith to build the "she shed," where my client goes to paint and have personal time. Fashioned after a cottage in Maine, the wood floors are painted in Farrow & Ball Teresa's Green and the walls in Pale Powder. The interior is decorated with wicker furniture from Soane and a large Moroccan screen, on which Charles Birdsong expertly hung blue-and-white Chinese export.

OPPOSITE: This folly was built for the client, an artist, for painting. The Soane wicker, handmade by only a few artisans in the U.K., is painted a pale robin's-egg blue. The new Swedish rug is from Abrash, and the screen and tables are from one of our favorite haunts—Ceylon et Cie. Both are conveniently located in Dallas.

ABOVE: I love a sectional to unify an awkward space. The Peter Fasano wallpaper provides a suitable backdrop for the Hodsoll McKenzie Indian flower print on the sofa. The Robert Kime ottoman in an ikat is perfect for putting your feet up. OPPOSITE: Conrad shades are the best for flexible coverage of a window. They are simple, yet elegant, and give privacy but allow light to come through. This is a wonderful spot for painting and reading.

PATTERN ON PATTERN

I started my career working for the venerable Joe Minton at Minton-Corley in Fort Worth, Texas. He taught me to pair imperfectly matched colors to create a tension that stimulates the eye and shakes things up. We are known for mixing patterned fabric on walls and furniture in a way that creates a chorus of color and life rather than discordant tones and prints. The trick is getting it just right. It is a delicate dance.

OPPOSITE AND RIGHT: For me, this bedroom is the ideal mix of styles and types of furnishings—Swedish, Indian, Chinese, Italian, and English. This is one of my favorite images—I love the reflection of the painting in the mirror. The Bennison Coromandel fabric is reminiscent of an Indian *palampore* that I love. It is a wonderful background for the blue-and-white Chinese export porcelain and the painted Venetian chair.

RIGHT: This bedroom is a good example of how the more you use one fabric in a space, the effect becomes "cocoonlike." Most people are afraid of using a busy fabric such as this everywhere. They think it will be overwhelming, but it is not. The Leontine Linens mixed with D. Porthault linens complete this dreamy room.

An Urban Oasis

*Siting a House in a Two-and-a-Half-Acre
Park-Like Setting in the Middle of Town*

I was hired to freshen this well-loved home of a family in Volk Estates, Dallas. Architect and designer David Anthony Easton designed this Spanish Colonial set on two and a half acres in the middle of this iconic neighborhood in 2001. The wife not only is a collector with discerning taste but is also involved in many civic organizations and causes in her community, and her husband is a successful businessman with many varied interests, from art to sport hunting and everything in between. They have four children and are finally empty nesters, but the family gathers often to return to their home. The well-planned and handsome architecture and the thoughtfully chosen materials provided the perfect backdrop for my work to begin. At every turn there was a treat to be treasured. From exquisite French and Italian antiques to beautiful rugs and wonderful porcelains, I had a treasure trove to work with.

I started with paint and lighting. The client had lived with warm colors for a decade and wished for lighter colors. For the living room, I pulled a soft blue green from the rug, which completely changed the room's appearance; the coolness of the blue green made the ochres and pinks in the rug appear clearer and brighter. With drapery the same color as the walls, accented with embroidery derived from a motif in the rug, the walls of the room seemed to recede, in effect highlighting its stellar views of the garden. All of the furniture was recovered in pale neutral solids or small prints to create a serene space. Details are important with plain fabrics, so custom trims were applied, and, in some cases, antique textiles were used. Art lighting was tucked inconspicuously into the beams so that the art and the porcelains look as if they are glowing. I added a few contemporary pieces, such as small tables, to complement the clients' contemporary art, making the room appear more relaxed.

Since the wife is whimsical and confident in her taste, for her powder bath she chose a Gracie paper with orange carp and lily pads that would intimidate most. I had Gracie design the honeycomb trellis to define the lavatory. Softly embroidered, simple café curtains allow more light into the room than the previous shutters.

Of all the rooms in the house, the screened porch is a favorite gathering place. Perfect for iced tea in the afternoons or late-night cocktails and cigars, it is the ideal spot for a relaxed visit. The client went all out for the bespoke wicker furniture from Soane—I appreciate handcrafted pieces since these arts are becoming lost arts. The room took on an Anglo-Indian feel with the fabrics and the marble Moorish table, and the handmade wool rug keeps it masculine and durable. Rooms have to be beautiful and comfortable—and in this case durable too. That's what makes a house a home.

OPPOSITE AND FOLLOWING SPREAD: This living room remains how David Easton had designed it but with a new color on the walls custom mixed by Barry A. Martin Painting Contractors and lighter fabrics on the upholstered pieces. The wall color fluctuates as the light changes during the day—from pale seafoam to celery. Contemporary art contrasts with traditional antiques. The spaced, pleated, custom lampshades with a cuff and trim by Charles Birdsong complete the beautiful lamps.

MIXING COLOR

Before settling on a color for any room, it is important to apply the paint on different walls and study how it changes throughout the day, from natural daylight to artificial nighttime light. The green in this living room fluctuates from apple to celery. My client wished to give her living room a fresh new take, but we wanted to be sensitive to the fine work that David Easton had done in this house, so I relied on my eye for a hue to replace the original yellow, ultimately choosing a soft blue green that changes color depending on how the light is hitting it.

OPPOSITE: Appliquéing fragments of an antique textile, from Antique Textiles in New York, to the back of this French chair adds a special detail.

RIGHT: When designing a room, the smallest things make a difference. Instead of trim, embroidery by Penn & Fletcher on the leading edge of this drapery brings the eye to all the colors and motifs of the rug from the floor to the walls, uniting the space. The *verre églomisé* frames on the Chinese junk watercolor and the pagoda lamp relate to one another in this vignette.

143

RIGHT: The Soane wicker furniture covered in Puka Prints is the perfect addition to the interior of this charming screened porch. The room is a casual, yet glamorous gathering place for enjoying the view as well as imbibing cocktails.

ABOVE: Gracie wallpaper and embroidered curtains by Julia B. are the perfect match for this powder room. Since this room faces the front of the house, the café curtains provide privacy but also allow light to fill the space. OPPOSITE: The clients' tables and art add a wonderful contrast to the Lisa Fine Textiles fabric on the chairs. Instead of one large table, a pair of tables allows easy access in a small room.

146

A Historic Beaux-Arts Estate

*A 1920s House and Orangery Tucked Along a
Creek Refreshing a Fabled Grand Dame*

It seems like everyone knows and loves this Hal Thompson–designed Beaux-Arts house, which is nestled along the banks of Turtle Creek in Dallas's Highland Park, even though it is hidden from the street and completely private in the back due to the creek. The house was originally built as a wedding gift for a prominent couple in the 1920s. My clients purchased it in the 1990s and have followed the original design to the letter of the law—adding on very sparsely. Prominent in business, both husband and wife sit on several boards, ranging from business to institutions and the arts. The wife is originally from New Orleans and has exceptional taste. Her style and graciousness are also evident in the interiors we've created over the years as they have raised their family. We've been working together for thirty years and are now in the process of redoing many rooms to reflect my clients' evolving tastes and preferences for style, as well as the changing needs of their family.

When we first decorated the house, Gracie murals were added to a mahogany-paneled living room. Today, we are lacquering the room in pale lavender. We are in the process of reupholstering furniture in creams and whites, giving the space a more transitional and less formal feel. The foyer with a staircase leading to the upstairs hallways, also lacquered white for years, with contemporary artwork lining the walls gives the house a youthful lift. For balance, we chose to keep the mahogany paneling in the dining room but added a high gloss for luminosity and lacquered the ceiling. An expansive mahogany table sits under a grand chandelier with a table filled with a collection of blue-and-white Hatcher porcelain.

In the library, which we originally decorated in lots of chintz and equestrian art that was in vogue at the time, we have switched gears entirely. One of the great features of the room is a large window looking out to the gardens and creek where ducks paddle and a canoe is docked. We recently lacquered the room the perfect shade of cantaloupe. It is a cozy space with comfortable furnishings. Artworks by Willem de Kooning and Helen Frankenthaler hang on the walls, and a beautiful Oushak carpet rests on the floor. We often instill pattern in a room with fabric but not in this case: the patterns in the room come from the rug and the artwork, an approach that makes everything feel more timelessly modern.

A loggia overlooking the terraces and gardens leads to a trellised room at the back of the house, which was original to the house. We restored the loggia with painstaking care, stripping down the walls to reach and create a color that is not quite blue and not quite gray. Today, this room doubles as either a stopping point or a passage to walkways leading to the newly built orangery filled with the intoxicating scent of citrus trees, which my clients often use for entertaining. We worked with architect Wilson Fuqua to create this structure, which was largely inspired by legendary orangeries, from the seventeenth-century model on the grounds of Versailles to the Edwin Lutyens–designed version at Hestercombe House in England. With a classical

OPPOSITE: This entry is original to the 1920s house. The only change has been the color of the paint, many times over the years. The walls are lacquered three subtle shades of white to accent the exquisite paneling. The center panels are the lightest and the stiles are the darkest, with the moldings the medium tone.

facade, French doors on three sides, and a vaulted ceiling painted in Farrow & Ball Skylight and walls in All White, the space has an ethereal note and feels as if you are sitting in the middle of a lush garden. We worked with Chateau Domingue in Houston, Texas, to design antique limestone floors, which we lined with laser-cut drains on the periphery to make watering the citrus trees easy.

We furnished the interior with a classical scheme, including symmetrical furniture arrangements and antique paintings that adorn the sitting area. We opted for a soft palette of neutrals and pale blues to create a sense of serenity. The furniture is a mixture of Swedish antiques and outdoor pieces from McKinnon and Harris covered in indoor-outdoor fabrics, so doors can be flung open and the space can seamlessly blend with the topiary gardens and creek trickling behind the property. Most of all the structure was designed for entertaining so, when not used for small luncheons or cocktails before dinner, the furniture is moved out and a long table can be set for large dinner parties, which was the case when our friend Bunny Williams last visited.

Back inside, moving upstairs, are the master suite and sitting room. My client is happiest in traditionally sized rooms, and this suite of rooms works in perfect tandem. In the sitting room, we upholstered most of the furniture in one of my favorite fabrics and installed a custom Holland and Sherry carpet. The bed is dressed in custom Leontine Linens. There are beautifully appointed his-and-hers baths and dressing rooms.

Down a long, lacquered white hallway where family photos hang are a guest room, the son's room, and the daughter's room. Each is completely different. For the guest room, we found a pair of campaign-style beds and hung canopies above them. The daughter's room is a standout with yards and yards of a pale pink and white Fortuny print fabric used everywhere. Chinese export porcelain adorns the walls and an Indian chest of drawers adds a little heft, keeping the space from being too sweet.

Though a work in progress, the interiors of this venerable house will soon be reimagined and, just as they did before, be ready to stand the test of time.

RIGHT: With a view of the garden, the library has been given a fresh look with the clients' choice of a painting by Willem de Kooning hanging over the fireplace and the Arne Jacobsen Egg chair. The painting influenced the color of the room, the fabrics, and the antique Oushak rug.

LACQUERED CEILINGS

Ceilings should never be ignored, and lacquering them will add height to a room. We typically choose a pale blue to give the illusion of sky or a shell pink for softening. Here, we wanted bold contrast, so the ceiling is lacquered in marshmallow white to boldly offset the polished mahogany walls. The result is stunning and gives the room the modern lift it needed.

OPPOSITE: The walnut-paneled dining room is a departure from the rest of this house, which is mostly painted in white and soft-colored lacquered walls. Blue-and-white striped silk drapery contrasts with the walls and coordinates with the clients' collection of blue-and-white Hatcher porcelain. Sisal rugs are smart and simple in this elegant room.

RIGHT: The monogramed linen chair slipcovers from Penn & Fletcher cover brown leather upholstered giltwood chairs. They allow the hostess to create more than one look in a chic dining room. The Italian giltwood blackamoor standing in the Chinese export fishbowl adds an unexpected focal point to the English sideboard.

ABOVE: Plaster brackets from Axel Vervoordt hold the clients' Chinese export collection of porcelain in the loggia. OPPOSITE: Scalloped lampshades by Charles Birdsong add whimsey to the Chinese lamps in the same room. Garden cloches retrofitted into bell jars relate to the garden outside. FOLLOWING SPREAD: The original trellis in the solarium was restored by the client to create this room. A marble Anglo-Indian table from Ceylon et Cie and the Martyn Lawrence Bullard pasha linen on the sofa are the finishing touches.

OPPOSITE: The master bedroom features a custom Chelsea Textiles embroidered canopied bed with exquisite Leontine Linens. I usually use white linens even if fabrics in the room have a cream background—they provide a crisp contrast. ABOVE: The sitting room off the bedroom has windows over the entry that were designed to catch the breezes in the hot seasons. The chair in the Colefax and Fowler chintz lives happily with the Puka Print from Tissus d'Hélène drapery, chair, and ottoman.

RIGHT: The combination of vintage tole beds with Robert Kime fabric on the bed drapery, Leontine Linens, and combed walls in a custom sunny yellow lacquer make a wonderful guest room. I always try to include a desk for guests to have a place to work.

OPPOSITE AND ABOVE: The clients' mahogany bed from the wife's youth was painted by Barry A. Martin Painting Contractors to create an idyllic guest room. Penn & Fletcher embroidery on the inside of the valence echoes the patterns of the Adelphi wallpaper and the Fortuny fabrics. Soft pink Christopher Spitzmiller lamps and Leontine Linens complement the look. An Indian chest and bone mirror and lamp from John Rosselli Antiques add an exotic touch.

RIGHT: Lanterns from Jamb London light this exquisite orangery designed by Wilson Fuqua. McKinnon and Harris furniture surround the John Rosselli tray table to allow people to enjoy this lovely room with its potted orange trees.

OPPOSITE: The client uses this room in the orangery for entertaining. Here, a table is draped in Penny Morrison Ashok fabric for a lunch for four. At night, a long table is set, complete with white linens and silver candlesticks for magical dinners for twelve or more.

FOLLOWING SPREAD: The painted bergère chairs covered in a pale blue stripe and Chinese coffee table change the room for a different look. I love the painted canvas panels the client found while antique shopping. I encourage my clients to shop for their homes—it makes everything much more personal.

A Bucolic Farm

*Conjuring a Childhood in Virginia
on a Gentleman's Farm*

When one of my favorite clients called me and said that she and her husband had purchased a farm near Athens, Texas, I was thrilled. Athens is a beautiful East Texas town with a rich history; it feels much different from Dallas and is only a little over an hour away. This residence, I was convinced, would offer an opportunity to create a true family retreat. The husband is from Virginia, and the oak trees and red soil reminded him of his home. The house had an interesting story, having been built by, of all people, a pair of famous wrestlers who just happened to be brothers; they eventually sold it to a highly regarded businessman and philanthropist whom my client knew personally.

The setting is bucolic with winding roads, bridges, a lake, and barns. The main house offers many rooms for all sorts of entertaining and generous porches for relaxing. Of course, as with many projects, it started out as a "fixer-upper"—we anticipated keeping most as is and just changing a few things. Then we got into the spirit of the house and decided that it needed to reflect more of the personalities of the young couple and their three children, as well as their varied interests. Entertaining friends was paramount, and the wife loves to cook for everyone herself. The couple is very involved in the arts in Dallas—only one of their many community involvements—and they collect contemporary and traditional art.

My client loves the process of creating a home but, because she is so busy, she delegates. She gives me direction and then asks me to come up with the schemes. Design boards were created and one evening over a bottle of very good wine we presented them to the client. Even after his tiring day at the office, the husband was so enthusiastic that I knew this was not only going to be a winning collaboration but a lot of fun as well. They stipulated that the project not drag on forever because they were excited to start using the home as soon as possible. We started with the Rose Cottage—aptly named because of the rose garden around it—and finished it in five months so they could stay there while watching the progress on the main house.

The Rose Cottage had one high-ceilinged great room and two adjacent bedrooms. We created a cozy area at one end of the room that could be for dining but with a sofa and comfortable chairs around the table—I like this approach when you need a room to provide several functions. They use this area for playing cards and games, catching up on emails on their laptops, and having leisurely evenings of conversation after dinner. The trick to making it comfortable is that the sofa and chairs needed to be a little taller for dining height. Keeping the colors soft and light meant that this room is equally as pleasing in the daytime as in the evening. In the room, we chose one Penny Morrison fabric with a palette of blues, yellows, and whites to drive our color choices for paint, coordinating fabrics, and rugs.

I used striped cotton rugs and natural fabrics to evoke a casual, relaxed feel. Painted furniture allowed me to place more furniture in the rooms without making them feel overcrowded. And, even in a cottage by the lake, beautiful linens and dressmaker details are still important. In the dining room, the client and I decided on a more eclectic feel, with large Arts and Crafts cabinets from Belgium filled with pottery from an important English ceramicist from the early twentieth century and an organic

OPPOSITE: The painted gingerbread door surround contrasts with an Indian paisley from Jasper in the entry of the Rose Cottage.
The painted case clock and furniture greet guests with a Swedish country feel.

wood table from designer Lars Bolander helping me achieve this. The midcentury Soane chairs added a clubby, elegant twist and allowed for long dinners because no one wanted to leave.

Most billiard rooms are in a playroom—or, many times, in basements. This one has windows on three sides with great views. Café curtains were chosen for window treatments to let the light in during the day and to see the stars at night. Comfortable 1930s leather club chairs surround an ottoman in an antique paisley for enjoying a cigar or strumming a few chords on the guitar, the husband's favorite instrument. Bar stools copied after Orkney chairs provide a place to perch while waiting for a turn at the table. This room is bright and cozy at the same time, a quiet comfortable place to read a book or a fun room for a boisterous game of pool. It is the true definition of a multiuse space.

All bedrooms have their own personality. I tried to make each unique by using different configurations of beds and specific colors through fabrics and wallpapers and art without making the rooms a theme or cliché. One room, which is aptly named the Three Bears Room, is perfect for children who want to have a slumber party or big girls who just want to continue the evening a little longer. Striped wallpaper with Swedish furniture and checked fabric keep it clean and simple. Pretty but easy-to-care-for bed linens make it luxurious, with Indian quilts adding a fun detail. The dioramas over the beds are a delight for children and adults alike. The master bedroom evokes an Anglo-Indian feel, which started with the purchase of the bed from Guinevere Antiques in London. Layered patterns and Indian textiles create an exotic but still light and simple retreat in this farmhouse. In all the bedrooms, the wallpaper, patterned rugs, and painted furniture were carefully selected by always keeping in mind that this home is a casual country house.

I feel that working in a country home is no different than working in a formal city setting: the construction must still be refined and an attention to detail retained. The materials might change but what stays the same is the integrity of the selected patterns and elements; these are what will achieve a quality design.

RIGHT: Pale blues and soft yellows combine with painted furniture, comfortable upholstery, and a striped rug to make this multiuse room light and bright. Since the cottage is next to a small lake, we placed the ship dioramas over the fireplace as a fun accent.

OPPOSITE: Comfortable club chairs around a dining table encourage guests to linger. We raised the seat height a few inches so they wouldn't sit too low around the table. The large mirror over the sofa visually extends the room.

ABOVE: For a guest room, double beds are more comfortable than twins, if the space allows. Always spend at least one night in your guest room to make sure all the amenities are there.
OPPOSITE: Primrose embroidered fabric from Chelsea Textiles frames the bamboo bed in the Rose Cottage's master bedroom. We use half canopies in rooms where a full canopy would interfere with watching TV or if the client is hesitant to have the bed enclosed with fabric. Full-height bed drapery raises the ceiling in a room with lower ceilings.

OPPOSITE: Painting the shiplap behind the rustic beams helps to lift the ceiling. Apple matting on floors is rustic and refined at the same time. ABOVE: You should always look at what a mirror is reflecting when hanging it in a room. The collection of bird prints is artfully reflected in the inlaid bone mirror between two quilted headboards. FOLLOWING SPREAD: We call this guest room the "Three Bears Room." The Chelsea Textiles headboards, upholstered in sunflower embroidered fabric, makes for a fun room for little or big girls sharing stories before bed. The Les Indiennes quilts are also printed with sunflowers.

EVERY HOUSE DESERVES DRESSMAKER DETAILS

We did not let the small size of the Rose Cottage take away from the opportunity to add our favorite dressmaker details: trim on upholstery, monogrammed linens, and handmade lampshades by designer Charles Birdsong. Details such as these make a house look finished.

OPPOSITE: An Indian bed from Guinevere Antiques in London is the focal point for this bedroom. Since many antique beds are high off the floor to catch the breeze, we needed bed steps. From John Rosselli Antiques, these steps make it easier to climb into bed. The Bennison fabric and wallpaper, Madeline Weinrib pillows, and Swedish daybed at the foot of bed add to this magical room.

RIGHT: Café curtains allow privacy yet light to fill a room that was a sleeping porch. A Oaxacan textile on the Bennison covered chair with a Chelsea Textiles pillow create a fun mix in this sunny corner.

OPPOSITE: Pattern on pattern on pattern. Painted furniture like this Regency chest of drawers adds charm in any room, especially when combined with a striped Elizabeth Eakins rug, Pierre Frey wallpaper, and Bennison fabric upholstered chair.

FOLLOWING SPREAD: Hand-blocked wallpaper and fabric from Bennison cover this bedroom in an all-over pattern. More pattern is added with D. Porthault linens. The Chelsea Textiles bench at the end of the bed is handy for placing suitcases or folding back the bedcovers at night.

My Home: A Restored 1920s Bungalow

Following My Own Best Practices for
Making a House Comfortable and Livable

My house is an open door to my four children and seven grandchildren, along with all of my pets as well as theirs. On top of that, my office is located in a back house on the property so there is always a lot of activity—it's not just my family coming and going but my friends, design team, and clients—who really are an extended family—being there as well. With this in mind, I designed a house that is simple but elegant and adapts easily to my lifestyle.

Built in the 1920s most likely as a caretaker's cottage, my American shingle-style house is one of the oldest in the neighborhood. The property, which includes a majestic tree, which conjures up rural New England rather than urban Dallas. The house may have been a mess when I purchased it, but I was drawn to how American it felt. There was no pretense to its honest exterior structure though the interior was all Tudor, with dark rooms, small leaded windows, and heavy plaster on the walls. A major renovation was required and, as I had already done for several clients, I turned to architect Wilson Fuqua for support. I'm a firm believer in getting the architecture right before starting to decorate; I'd rather have plain curtains on perfect windows than disguise the problem windows with elaborate curtains. When we opened up the walls, we found that the windows, which had been patched over the years, went all of the way to the floor.

Now, you enter the house through a solid front door painted in Farrow & Ball's Studio Green in a high-gloss finish into a foyer with a wall of steel windows that lend a modern touch and allow tremendous light into the house. On the floors, we installed a marble pattern in Ann Sacks tiles that is traditionally elegant yet incredibly practical for well-trafficked areas. To respect the cottage aspect, we used beadboard on the heightened ceiling painted pale blue and added a transom entry with pocket doors leading to the living room. The entry space, with morning sun, doubles as a sun porch or resting space, so I furnished it with a welcoming bench backed with antique-textile pillows, vintage rattan furniture, Indian-style tables, a large oak table for books, planted urns, and a blue-and-white porcelain lamp.

One of my secret weapons is the design stylist Charles Birdsong, who also creates the beautiful bespoke lampshades that are a hallmark in all of my projects. My house is no exception. It is a creative canvas—with the furniture, artwork, objects, and Charlie's artistic medium, they find new interpretations under his creative genius. I like to establish one carefully blended color palette that starts at the front door and works its way through the interior spaces and out the back door. The palette stays the same, but the groupings and hangings seem to constantly change with Charlie.

OPPOSITE: An eclectic mix of porcelain tops the lacquered Queen Anne highboy in the dining room. Picture lights on paintings create a glow in a room, especially at night.
FOLLOWING SPREAD: A converted front porch becomes an inviting entry, thanks to the large steel window and Ann Sacks marble mosaic floors. A mix of Provençal French pieces, a midcentury Italian cane chair, and Moroccan table is an unexpected surprise in a New England–style house.

IT'S ALL IN THE MIX

I decorated my house with an eye to ease and comfort, combining everything I love most: blue and white, Indian, Moroccan, traditional antiques, classic still-life paintings, and contemporary art. Mixing periods and styles is a delicate balance but when done well, it produces timeless rooms you never tire of.

OPPOSITE: A painting by my dear friend, Mary McMahon Crain, is the focal point of the entry behind a table filled with blue-and-white porcelain and faux bamboo benches, upholstered from an Indian bedspread.

RIGHT: Displayed above the table are several styles of blue-and-white pottery and porcelain—from Chinese export and faience to majolica and delft.

The living room features many of the paintings I have collected over the years—from nineteenth-century still lifes to contemporary works—hung salon style with comfortable upholstery and lots of small chairs that can be moved around and get tucked into spots depending on how I'm using the room. I have hosted weddings, birthday parties, museum fundraisers, and holidays in this house. The rooms expand when needed or become intimate when it is just two friends sharing a drink in front of the fireplace. The little slipper chairs, upholstered in my favorite Sister Parish fabric, move around the most. The ceilings in this room are not tall, so to cheat the eye and maximize the floor-to-ceiling windows we used short valances and simple linen curtains.

A transom entry leads to the dining room in which I was able to preserve antique murals depicting a shipping scene that were originally painted by interior designer and artist Nena Claiborne. They survived a fire at my former home, and I was so relieved I could work with Barry A. Martin Painting Contractors to salvage and enhance them to fit all the way around the room. I continued beadboard in the foyer on the fireplace wall and painted it and the chair rail, which was added, in Farrow & Ball French Gray. A striped rug from Elizabeth Eakins keeps the room from skewing too formal. Like the living room, the ceiling is lacquered in a pale blue.

As I mentioned, I entertain a lot and love to cook and arrange flowers. My kitchen and mudroom were designed with generous work spaces, deep sinks, and ample storage. The kitchen is tiled in antique delft tile from Solar Antique Tiles. The family room extends from the kitchen and spans the back of the house with large window bays. This is "pet central," so nothing in here is too precious—it can all easily be cleaned or replaced. Many large paintings hang in this room, including my most coveted contemporary piece, the Julio Larraz watermelon painting, which I took out a loan to purchase when I was first starting out. As I tell my clients, buy the best you can afford; invest in quality, and you won't regret it. A round Eero Saarinen table with bentwood chairs seems to float under the oil painting with a view to the pool and backyard with my chickens in their coop around the corner.

RIGHT: A large midcentury coffee table from Mallet in London anchors the living room. Sitting on top of an antique rug and apple matting from Stark Carpet, this table provides a surface for collections, piles of books, and a place to set hors d'oeuvres. The artwork is hung salon style, taking advantage of every inch of the walls.

PRECEDING SPREAD: Transoms above doors lift the eye and provide extra light in rooms. The glass pocket doors when closed give a glimpse into the dining room, which is especially magical when the table is set and candles are lit.

LEFT: The contemporary painting by David Bates of his dog, Clovis, is the focal point of my dining room because Clovis resembles my beloved dog, Eloise, a bird dog. There is no better ambience for a dining room than a fireplace. This one looks like painted wood but is actually painted plaster.

ABOVE: I love this vase, with its hand-painted flowers on amethyst glass—a popular Victorian-era style—because it was given to me by a wonderful client and friend. My favorite florist, Margaret Ryder, has filled it with apple-green viburnum. OPPOSITE: Light from several sources, such as chandeliers, sconces, and architectural lighting, is important in a dining room. A summer supper table is set with vintage and new cabbage dinnerware and vintage D. Porthault linens. Softly lit lamps and an abundance of candles line the room and provide different levels of light.

OPPOSITE: Scenic murals add depth to a room. This detail of the painted canvas by Nina Claiborne in the dining room was saved from my previous home that was destroyed by fire.
ABOVE: Apple-green Christopher Spitzmiller lamps flank blue-and-white porcelain on the Georgian sideboard in the dining room's bay window.

The little center room beneath the stair hall to the second floor has taken on many Charles Birdsong transformations. It is currently a library I use mostly at night, and also functions as an adjunct sitting area for the guest bedroom suite on the first floor, which has a princess-and-the-pea canopy bed. It is a vintage Albert Hadley design, dressed in two Lisa Fine Textiles and custom Leontine Linens. Pretty linens are my biggest weakness, and the large walk-in closet in this room offers extra storage for my vast collection. I hung the vintage mirror from John Rosselli & Associates above the bed because I think older things give a room character. Not enough younger designers look to the past, and that is a mistake because there's so much meaning there, and much to be learned. I also love historic Adelphi paper hangings for this reason, and this one is a reproduction of a pattern from 1760. To keep it fresh, I added rattan tray tables from Serena & Lily and lampshades from Pottery Barn.

My bedroom and a second guest room are upstairs along with a charming attic-style playroom for my grandchildren, designed by the beloved Dallas architect Charles Dilbeck. The master bedroom has an Anglo-Indian motif with a canopy bed from John Rosselli & Associates in bone and ebony covered in multiple linen patterns from D. Porthault. Along with the family room, it is the room where my pets feel right at home. I nabbed a Moroccan screen at the Round Top Antiques Fair for practically free and had it cut in half to flank both sides of the bed. Since I love tennis, Charles Birdsong designed shades with trim reminiscent of my tennis skirts for vintage turquoise lamps. The upstairs guest room is papered in a cheerful turquoise ikat pattern from Quadrille Fabrics, which I have always loved since my days at Minton-Corley in 1974, with a well-made bed dressed in monogrammed Leontine Linens pillows and D. Porthault linens.

Though not fancy, we haven't sacrificed elegance and comfort and livability. I think my family and friends would agree that everyone feels at home here—even the chickens.

LEFT: The large still-life painting of a watermelon by Julio Larraz anchors
this sitting room, as it has in all my homes. I tell my clients, "Buy what you love
and you will keep it forever."

RIGHT: A favorite gathering spot in the family room is the welcoming Eero Saarinen table surrounded by chairs from *Design Within Reach*, covered in an Elizabeth Eakins fabric, which are set on a Madeline Weinrib rug. The blue-and-white color scheme is simple and neutral to live with—especially if you are around colors all day as I am.

OPPOSITE: In the kitchen, upper cabinets were eliminated to create an open feel. A large steel window is a wonderful sunny spot for nurturing my topiary addiction. The Urban Electric lanterns with white glass provide great light over the island without glare. ABOVE: The butler's pantry with the farm sink is perfect for arranging flowers, and doubles as a bar for parties.

ABOVE: This John Dickenson table has followed me for forty-five years—from my first apartment to my current house. Now, the table resides in this stair hall where I added bookshelves, library lights with Fermoie shades, and a banquette with slipper chairs covered in a Sister Parish fabric. I can easily transform this lovely spot for small dinners by replacing it and the slipper chairs with a round draped table and chairs. OPPOSITE: Wooden pegs come in handy in a busy mudroom, and the horizontal painted shiplap adds interest and visual contrast. Hardware is jewelry for the home. This P. E. Guerin rim lock dresses up an otherwise ordinary door.

ABOVE: My favorite stylist and designer, Charles Birdsong, found these lamps and then designed the shades for my bedside tables. Charles hung Moroccan screens behind them. I would have never thought of that. I've learned how important it is to bring in experts. OPPOSITE: This fantastic Indian bone bed is from John Rosselli Antiques. Add D. Porthault linens and it makes a place for the sweetest dreams. The ottoman is covered in antique textiles and holds all the reading material I never seem to get around to reading.

OPPOSITE: Charles Birdsong used a collection of Indian miniature watercolors, a bone inlaid mirror, and bone box from John Rosselli Antiques to create the perfect vignette in my bedroom. ABOVE: I love having houseguests. This bed canopy with Lisa Fine Textiles fabrics, Leontine Linens, and the "Besos" (or "Kisses") pillow, from my friends at Mi Golondrina, hopefully makes them want to linger.

Acknowledgments

Every day I am reminded that I have the best clients in the world. This book has been an opportunity for me to celebrate each of them and the creative collaborations I have enjoyed throughout my career.

I honestly could have never accomplished such a feat without the excellent support of the team behind this book. Thank you to Rizzoli International Publications' publisher, Charles Miers, for his unerring vision and to Sandy Gilbert Freidus for her careful eye and knack for keeping everyone on track. I feel lucky to have an editor who cares so deeply about her authors and the finished product.

A thank-you to Dan Lori of the Lori Group for his stunning creative direction. I have also loved working with such gifted photographers who amaze me with their ability to interpret my work in a way I had not considered before.

I am especially indebted to Chesie Breen, who is not only a wonderful friend but also a respected public relations consultant. She was instrumental in working with me on the book—it would have never happened without Chesie's encouragement.

I thank Bunny Williams and John Rosselli, my dear friends whom I consider family. I can think of no two better suited to write my book's foreword. I am grateful for their love and support.

To my wonderful staff, in particular Rachel Cooper, who left no detail unturned.

Lastly, this book is dedicated to my children—Callie, Lindsay, Sam, and Maggie—and to my late husband, Bill Hudson. Every day is a gift because of each of them.

Resources

As an interior designer, I feel incredibly lucky to have access to so many talented resources.
Here are a few that I work with most frequently.

ANTIQUES DEALERS

Antique Textiles Collections
antiquetextilescollections.com
212-535-0055

Ceylon et Cie
shop.michellenussbaumer.com
214-742-7632

George N Antiques
georgenantiques.com
212-935-4005

Gerald Bland
geraldblandinc.com
212-987-8505

Guinevere
guinevere.co.uk
+44 (0) 20 7736 2917

John Rosselli Antiques
johnrosselliantiques.com
212-750-0060

Malachite
malachitehome.com
504-754-0066

Nick Brock Antiques
nickbrockantiques.com
214-828-0624

Parc Monceau
parcmonceauatl.com
404-467-8107

Ware Porter & Co.
wareporter.com
504-267-3868

Wolf Hall Antique Collective
wolfhallantiques.com
214-533-9299

ARCHITECTS

Bruno Lafourcade
architecture-lafourcade.com
+33 (0) 4 90 92 10 14

**J. Wilson Fuqua &
Associates Architects**
wilsonfuqua.com
214-528-4663

Jay Smith Architect
jaysmitharchitect.com
214-298-5098

John B. Murray Architect
Jbmarchitect.com
212-242-8600

ARCHITECTURAL ANTIQUES

A & R Asta
astafireplaces.com
212-750-3364

Chateau Domingue
chateaudomingue.com
713-961-3444

Pittet Architecturals
pittetarch.com
214-651-7999

ARTISANS

Charles Birdsong
214-695-3071

Jeff Hogan
972-415-3112

Mita Bland
mitacorsinibland.com

EMBROIDERY

Holland and Sherry
interiors.hollandandsherry.com
469-249-6422 (Dallas)

Julia B.
Juliab.com
707-756-3930

Leontine Linens
leontinelinens.com
504-899-7833

Penn & Fletcher, Inc.
pennandfletcher.com
212-239-6868

FABRICS / WALLCOVERINGS

Adelphi Paper Hangings
adelphipaperhangings.com
518-284-9066

Aleta Ltd.
aletaonline.com
+44 (0) 20 7228 9676

Bennison Fabrics
bennisonfabrics.com
214-744-1544

Chelsea Textiles
chelseatextiles.com
212-758-0005

**Claremont Furnishing
Fabrics Co.**
claremontfurnishing.com
212-486-1252

deGournay
degournay.com
212-564-9750

Gracie
graciestudio.com
214-749-5777 (Dallas)

Jasper Fabrics
michaelsmithinc.com
310-315-3028

John Rosselli and Associates
johnrosselli.com
212-593-2060

Les Indiennes
lesindiennes.com
518-828-2811

Lisa Fine Textiles
lisafinetextiles.com

Sister Parish Design
sisterparishdesign.com
1-800-970-3366

FLOORING

Ann Sacks
annsacks.com
214-742-8453 (Dallas)

Doris Leslie Blau
dorislieblau.com
212-586-5511

Elizabeth Eakins, Inc.
elizabetheakins.com
212-628-1950

Stark
starkcarpet.com
214-742-8252 (Dallas)

FURNITURE

Bunny Williams Home
bunnywilliamshome.com
212-935-5930

Fabulous Things
fabulousthingsatlanta.com
404-350-0916

McKinnon and Harris
mckinnonharris.com
804-358-2385

Oomph
oomphhome.com
203-518-8068

Soane Britain
soane.co.uk
+44 (0) 20 7730 6400

HARDWARE

P. E. Guerin
peguerin.com
212-243-5270

HOME DECOR

Ellis Hill
ellis-hill.com
214-520-6108

LIGHTING

Cele Johnson
214-651-1645

Charles Edwards
charlesedwards.com
+44 (0) 20 7736 8490

Christopher Spitzmiller, Inc.
christopherspitzmiller.com
212-563-3030

Coleen & Company
coleenandcompany.com
310-606-2050

Jamb Ltd.
jamb.co.uk
+44 (0) 20 7730 2122

Joseph Richter, Inc.
josephrichterinc.com
212-421-0673

STK Designs
214.632.3277

The Urban Electric Co.
urbanelectric.com
843-723-8140

PAINT RESOURCES

**Barry A. Martin
Painting Contractors**
barrymartinpainting.com
214-350-0723

Donald Kaufman Color
donaldkaufmancolor.com
201-568-2226
(Color Factory)

Farrow & Ball
farrow-ball.com
1-888-511-1121

Pierre Finkelstein
fauxbrushes.com
1-888-328-9278

UPHOLSTERY

Bespoke
bespokefinefurniture.com
713-877-9526

Cameron Collection
cameroncollection.com
214-752-4421

De Angelis
deangelisltd.com
516-723-3101

Kisabeth Furniture
kisabethfurniture.com
214-745-1340 (Dallas)

page 2 No sunroom is complete without a garden stool. For this solarium, we covered a Parsons table with wallpaper to add yet another layer of pattern to a sophisticated room.

page 4 The papier-mâché folly under a Swedish table references the leaded rondel window.

pages 6, 8–9 For the 2015 Kips Bay Decorator Showhouse, I designed a bedroom inspired by Indian motifs. I started by making a list of my most trusted resources—Adelphi, John Rosselli Antiques, Claremont, Penn & Fletcher, Barry Martin Painting Contractor, Stark Carpet, and Leontine Linens.

I commissioned artist Mita Bland to create watercolors for some of my favorite rooms for the following pages.

page 216 I like to mix styles and periods. Here, a nineteenth-century bureau anchors a contemporary Lucite lamp with a custom Charles Birdsong lampshade, a collection of blue-and-white porcelain, and an Indian mirror.

page 218 The large blue-and-white tole jar in the window adds another graphic detail to the bedroom.

page 220 I often collaborate with floral designer Margaret Ryder, and love that she used candlesticks by artist Bjørn Wiinblad as vases for peonies, my favorite flower.

page 222 I found this antique giltwood girandole at auction and worked with Charles Birdsong to wire it for modern use.

Credits

First published in the United States of America in 2019 by

Rizzoli International Publications, Inc.
300 Park Avenue South
New York, New York 10010

www.rizzoliusa.com

Text © 2019 Cathy Kincaid
Foreword: Bunny Williams and John Rosselli

Publisher: Charles Miers
Editor: Sandra Gilbert Freidus
Editorial Assistance: Elizabeth Smith and Rachel Selekman
Production Manager: Barbara Sadick
Managing Editor: Lynn Scrabis

Design: Dan Lori of The Lori Group

Printed in China

2020 2021 2022 / 10 9 8 7 6 5 4 3

ISBN: 978-0-8478-6356-3
Library of Congress Control Number: 2019937992

Visit us online:
Facebook.com/RizzoliNewYork
Twitter: @Rizzoli_Books
Instagram.com/RizzoliBooks
Pinterest.com/RizzoliBooks
Youtube.com/user/RizzoliNY
Issuu.com/Rizzoli